My First Pocket Guide

WYOMING

By Carole Marsh

Correlates with Wyoming's SSCPS Social Studies Content and Performance Standards

The WYOMING Experience

The GALLOPADE GANG

Carole Marsh
Bob Longmeyer
Chad Beard
Cecil Anderson
Steven Saint-Laurent
Jill Sanders
Kathy Zimmer
Terry Briggs
Pat Newman
Billie Walburn
Jackie Clayton
Pam Dufresne
Cranston Davenport
Lisa Stanley
Antoinette Miller
Victoria DeJoy
Al Fortunatti
Shery Kearney

Published by GALLOPADE INTERNATIONAL

www.wyomingexperience.com
800-536-2GET • www.gallopade.com

Other Wyoming Experience Products

- The Wyoming Experience!
- The BIG Wyoming Reproducible Activity Book
- The Wyoming Coloring Book
- My First Book About Wyoming!
- Wyoming "Jography": A Fun Run Through Our State
- Wyoming Jeopardy!: Answers and Questions About Our State
- The Wyoming Experience! Sticker Pack
- The Wyoming Experience! Poster/Map
- Discover Wyoming CD-ROM
- Wyoming "Geo" Bingo Game
- Wyoming "Histo" Bingo Game

A Word From the Author... (okay, a few words)...

Hi!

Here's your own handy pocket guide about the great state of Wyoming! It really will fit in a pocket—I tested it. And it really will be useful when you want to know a fact you forgot, to bone up for a test, or when your teacher says, "I wonder . . ." and you have the answer—instantly! Wow, I'm impressed!

Get smart, have fun!

Carole Marsh

Wyoming Basics explores your state's symbols and their special meanings!

Wyoming Geography digs up the what's where in your state!

Wyoming History is like traveling through time to some of your state's great moments!

Wyoming People introduces you to famous personalities and your next-door neighbors!

Wyoming Places shows you where you might enjoy your next family vacation!

Wyoming Nature - no preservatives here, just what Mother Nature gave to Wyoming!

All the real fun stuff that we just HAD to save for its own section!

Who Named You?

Wyoming's official state name is...

Wyoming

Word Definition

OFFICIAL: appointed, authorized, or approved by a government or organization

Statehood: July 10, 1890

Wyoming was the 44th state to join the Union.

Wyoming will be on a state-commemorative quarter starting in the year 2007. Look for it in cash registers everywhere!

What's In A Name?

Wyoming got its name from the Delaware Indian phrase *meche-weami-ing*, meaning "land of mountains and valleys alternating."

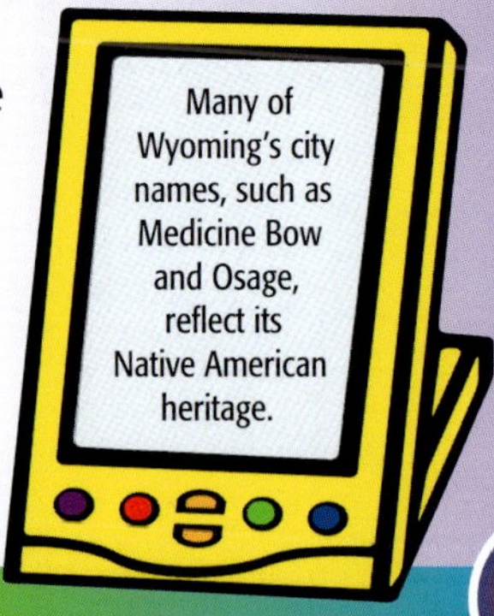

WHO Are You Calling Names?

State Nicknames

Wyoming is not the only name by which the state is recognized. Like many other states, Wyoming has some nicknames, official or unofficial!

The Equality State
(official)

The Cowboy State
(unofficial)

State Capital: Cheyenne

Established 1867

Since 1890

Cheyenne started as one of the "tent cities" that followed General Dodge as he pushed the nation's first Transcontinental Railroad westward in 1867. The tents gave way to rough cabins when Union Pacific established a winter camp and the U.S. cavalry established a protective post nearby.

The ceiling of each chamber in the capitol is stained glass with the state seal in the center.

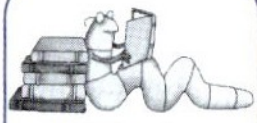

Word Definition

CAPITAL: a town or city that is the official seat of government
CAPITOL: the building in which the government officials meet

Who's in Charge Here?

Wyoming's GOVERNMENT has three branches:

- **EXECUTIVE**: A governor, secretary of state, state auditor, state superintendent of public instruction, and state treasurer
- **LEGISLATIVE**: Two Houses: The Senate (30 members) House of Representatives (64 members)
- **JUDICIAL**: Supreme Court (one chief justice and five associate justices) District Court County Court

The number of legislators is determined by population, which is counted every ten years; the numbers above are certain to change as Wyoming grows and prospers!

State Flag

Wyoming's current state flag was adopted in 1917. It features a bison with the state seal in the middle of a blue field, surrounded by a white and red band. The blue stands for the color of the sky and mountains; the white stands for purity and uprightness over Wyoming; and the red symbolizes Wyoming's Indian heritage and the blood the pioneers shed while claiming the land.

As you travel throughout Wyoming, count the times you see the Wyoming flag! Look for it on government vehicles, too!

State Seal

The state seal of Wyoming features a woman standing before a banner that reads "Equal Rights."

On either side of the woman are two pillars, each with scrolls that proclaim Wyoming's major economic strengths.

The men on either side of the pillars represent the mining and livestock industries. The burning lamps on the pillar symbolize the Light of Knowledge, and the shield, star, and eagle represent Wyoming's sovereignty and dedication to the Union. The dates 1869 and 1890 represent the territory and statehood dates, and the number 44 identifies Wyoming as the 44th state to enter the Union.

Word Definition

MOTTO: a sentence, phrase, or word expressing the spirit or purpose of an organization or group

State Motto

Wyoming's state motto is...

Equal Rights

Wyoming was the first state in U.S history to officially grant women the right to vote, hold offices, own land, and earn equal wages.

Western Meadowlark

This yellow, black, and white songbird has a "V" on its yellow breast.

The western meadowlark is very similar to the eastern meadowlark. However, the western meadowlark's song is louder and more flutelike.

Cottonwood

The cottonwood traveled west with the settlers. It was the only tree willing to grow in some spots on the prairies. The pioneers used this hardy and fast-growing tree to make their cabins, barns, corrals, and churches.

Indian Paintbrush

A lovelier flower
on earth was
never sown.
—William
Wordsworth

The Indian paintbrush grows in meadows and prairies and along roadsides from coast to coast. It stands upright and can grow to be 3 feet (91 centimeters) in height. Its color ranges from bright red to orange to yellow. The small leaves that surround the flowers are what actually give the plant its brilliant color.

Native American myth says this flower sprang up from magic paintbrushes dipped in the fiery colors of the sunset!

RIDDLE:
If the state flower got mixed up with the state bird, what would you have?

ANSWER: An Indian who likes to paint meadows with his paintbrush!

Bison have poor eyesight but good hearing and an excellent sense of smell. They can move at speeds of up to 35 miles (56 kilometers) per hour.

The American bison is a symbol of the West. They are sometimes called "buffalo," although they are not in the same family as the Asian and African buffalo. The difference is the large shoulder hump of the bison.

The bison's fur varies with the season, changing color and character. Their most obvious weapon is the horns that both male and female have. Other defenses include their head that can be used as a battering ram and their hind legs which can kill or maim. Their behavior is unpredictable. They appear peaceful but can attack anything, without warning or apparent reason.

TRICERATOPS

This rhinoceros-like dinosaur wandered the plains. It was a plant-eater that weighed between 7 to 9 tons (7.7 to 9.9 metric tons). Its head had three large horns, a big neck frill of solid bone, and a sharp parrot-like beak. The large horns, massive body, and powerful tail were all powerful weapons for the Triceratops.

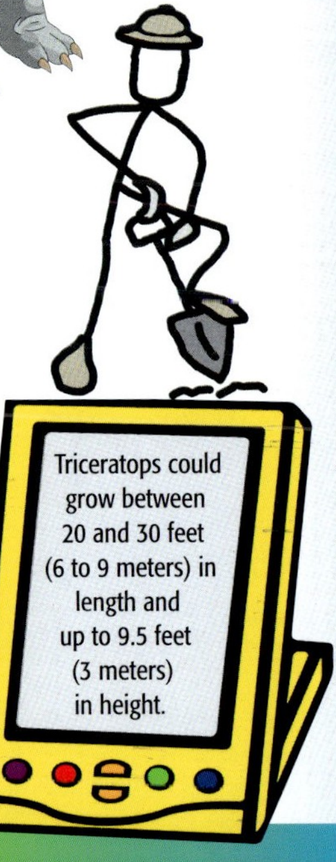

KNIGHTIA

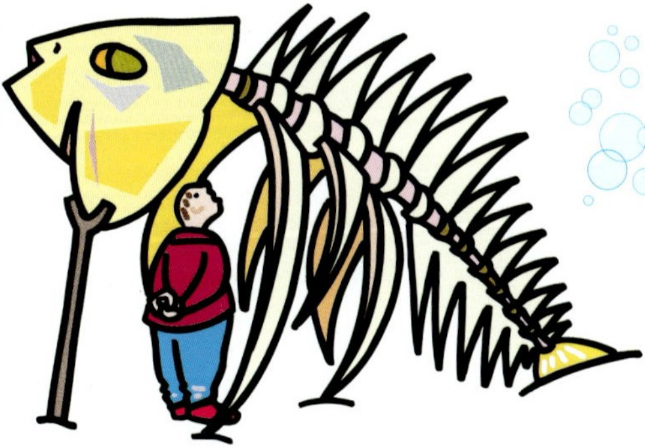

This fossil is a type of prehistoric fish, related to today's herrings. It lived 50 million years ago in a freshwater lake in what is now southwestern Wyoming. Scientists are not sure of the cause of its extinction. All they know is that the fish died suddenly and in large groups.

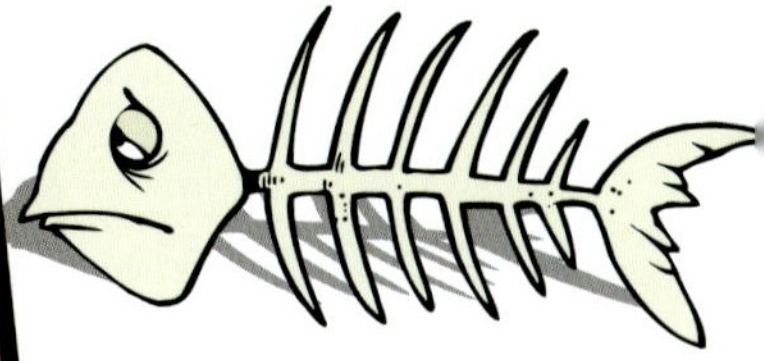

State Song

"Wyoming"

lyrics by Charles E. Winter, music by G.E. Knapp

The Wyoming state song was adopted in 1955. The first verse begins as follows:

In the far and mighty West,

Where the crimson sun seeks rest,

There's a growing splendid State that lies above

On the breast of this great land;

Where the massive Rockies stand,

There's Wyoming young and strong, the State I love!

Jade

Jade is valued for its color and freedom from cracks. It should have a greasy appearance when polished. Colors of jade range from many shades of green to yellow, red, black, and white. The most highly valued jade is lavender. This is also the rarest form of the stone.

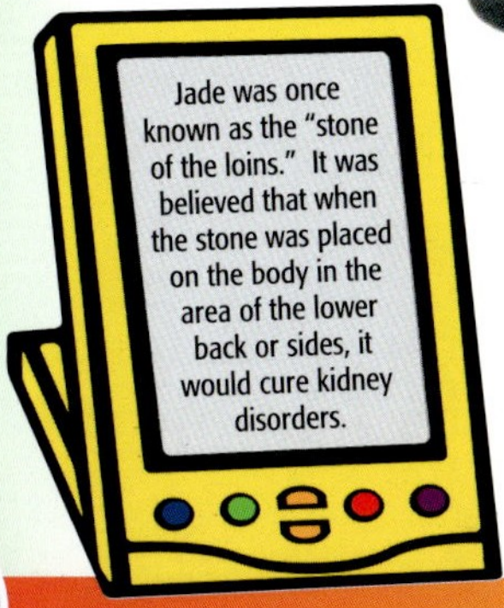

Horned Lizard

Horned lizards are often incorrectly called "horned toads." They have short horns that project from their head. They are well adapted to heat and also to extreme cold. Their body is short and flattened, which makes it able to absorb much of the sun's heat. They are quite small—only 3 to 6 inches (8 to 15 centimeters) in length. Horned lizards use their heads, limbs, and ribs to burrow.

Cutthroat Trout

State Fish

The back and sides of the cutthroat trout are lightly spotted. There is a red or reddish-orange slash under their throats. That's why they are called "cutthroat." They prefer the same habitat as rainbow trout and are found in similar areas.

Wyoming Cutthroat Trout

Put a trout filet on foil. Drizzle with lemon juice. Sprinkle with salt and pepper. Add shredded smoked ham and broil fish until done.

The State of Wyoming

"... If they ever saw a sunrise on a mountain morning or watched those cotton candy clouds go by then they'd know why I live beneath these western skies ..."
— Chris LeDoux

State Location

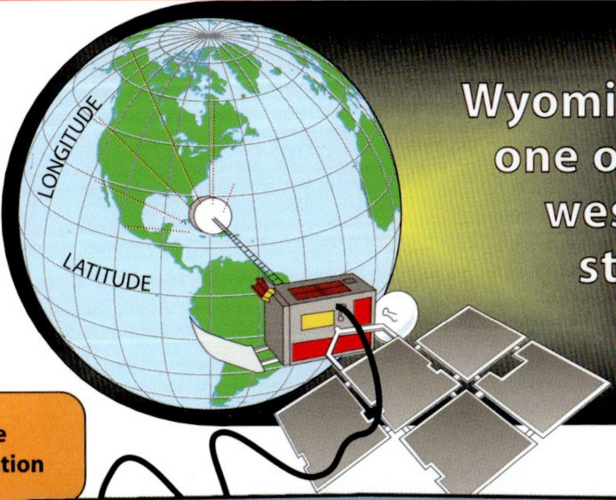

Wyoming is one of the western states.

State Location

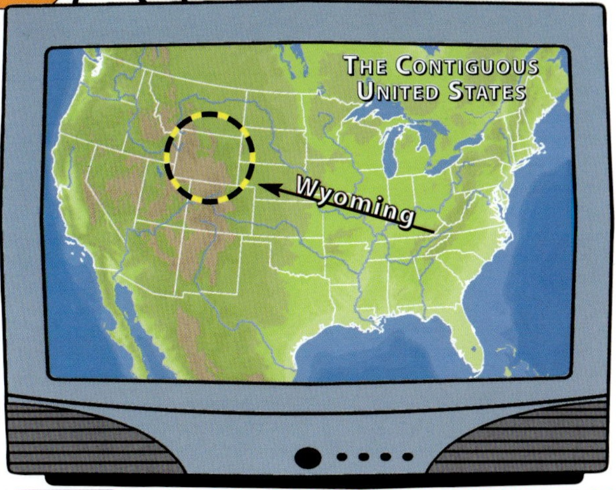

Word Definition

LATITUDE: Imaginary lines which run horizontally east and west around the globe

LONGITUDE: Imaginary lines which run vertically north and south around the globe

On The Border!

These border Wyoming:

States: Montana, South Dakota, Nebraska, Colorado, Utah, Idaho

---

Besides Colorado, Wyoming is the only state whose borders are formed by four straight lines.

I'll Take the Low Road...

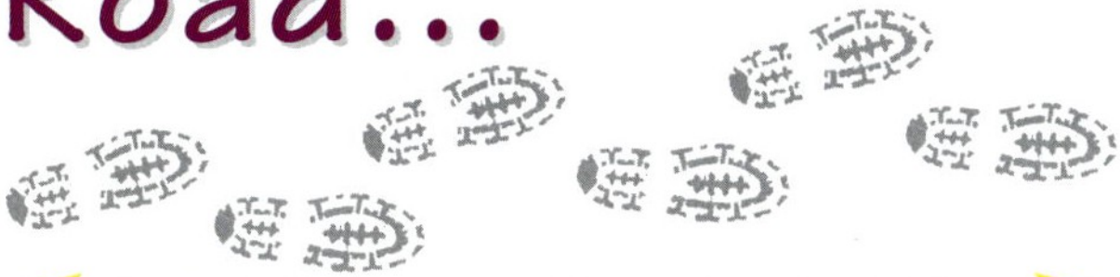

East-West, North-South, Area

Wyoming stretches 280 miles (451 kilometers from north to south—or south to north. Either way, it's a long drive!

Total Area: Approximately 97,819 square miles (253,331 square kilometers)
Land Area: Approximately 97,105 square miles (251,482 square kilometers)

Wyoming is 362 miles (583 kilometers) from east to west—or west to east. Either way, it's *still* a long drive!

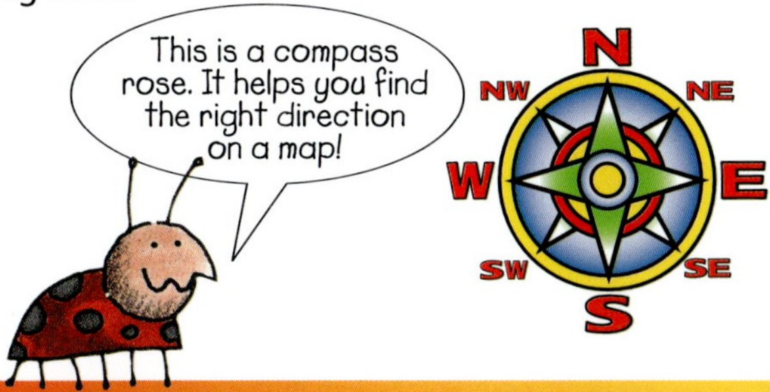

You Take the High Road!

HIGHEST POINT

GANNETT PEAK—13,804 FEET (4,207 METERS)

Gannett Peak is surrounded by five glaciers—Dinwoody, Gooseneck, Gannett, Mammoth, and Minor.

LOWEST POINT

BELLE FOURCHE RIVER IN CROOK COUNTY—3,100 FEET (945 METERS)

I'm County-ing on You!

Wyoming is divided into 23 counties.

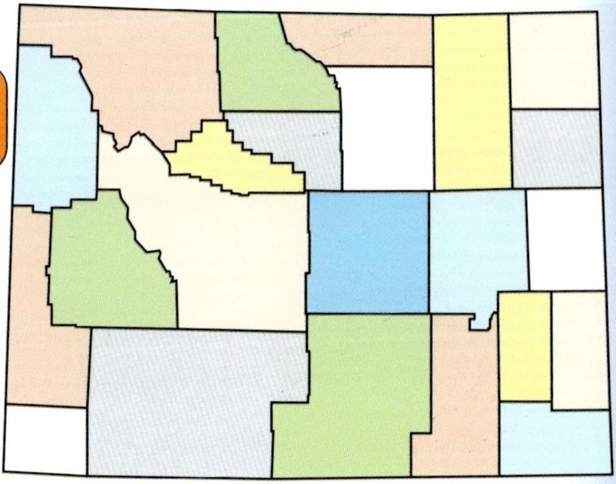

Word Definition

COUNTY:
an administrative subdivision of a state or territory

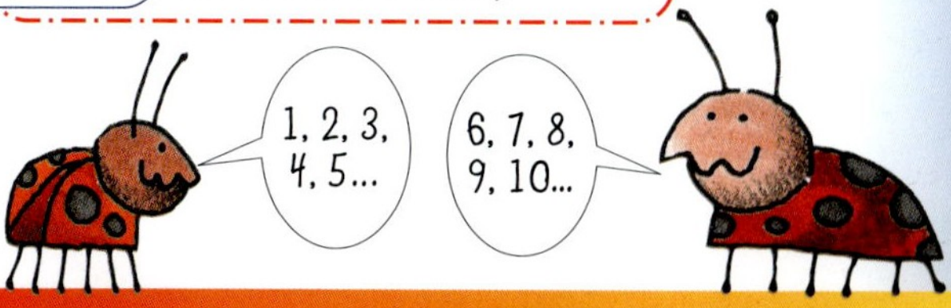

Natural Resources

It's All Natural!

Forests make up about 9,966,000 acres (4,033,240 hectares) in Wyoming.

Natural Resources

Word Definition

NATURAL RESOURCES: things that exist in or are formed by nature

Minerals and rocks:

Coal
Natural Gas
Petroleum
Uranium

Weather, Or Not?!

Wyoming's temperatures average 19°F (-7°C) in the winter and 67°F (19°C) in the summer.

Highest temperature: 115°F (46°C), Basin, August 8, 1983 and Diversion Dam, July 15, 1988

°F=Degrees Fahrenheit °C=Degrees Celsius

Lowest temperature: -63°F (-53°C), Moran, February 9, 1933

Generally, Wyoming has a cool, dry climate. The dry air makes the winters' cold temperatures feel less severe.

BACK ON TOP

Wyoming's topography includes:

Rocky Mountains—consists of three subdivisions known as the Southern Rocky Mountains, the Wyoming Basins, and the Middle Rocky Mountains; Continental Divide passes through the Wyoming Basins

Great Plains—upland plateau, broken up by low hills and isolated buttes; cover eastern third of the state

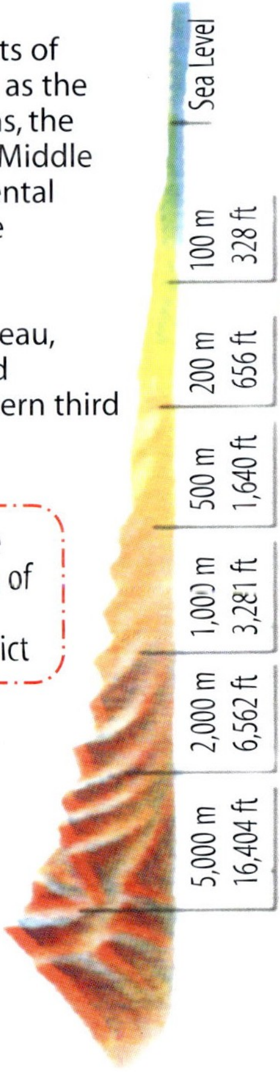

Word Definition

TOPOGRAPHY: the detailed mapping of the features of a small area or district

The Continental Divide marks the dividing line between the country's westward-flowing and eastward-flowing rivers.

King of the Hill

Tetons
Bighorn
Owl Creek
Gros Ventre
Wind River
Laramie
Medicine Bow
Sierra Madre

Down The River

Here are some of Wyoming's major rivers:

- **Missouri**
- **Snake**
- **Yellowstone**
- **Bighorn**
- **Powder**
- **Belle Fourche**
- **North Platte**
- **Green**
- **Sweetwater**
- **Horse**
- **Shoshone**

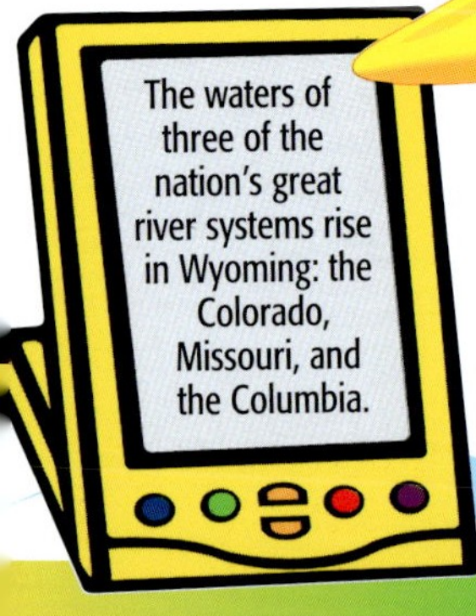

Gone Fishin'

- Yellowstone Lake
- Jackson Lake
- Shoshone Lake
- Lewis Lake
- Fremont Lake
- Boulder Lake
- Flaming Gorge Reservo
- Bighorn Lake
- Buffalo Bill Reservoir

Wyoming's two largest lakes are Yellowstone Lake in Yellowstone National Park and Jackson Lake in Grand Teton National Park.

Word Definition

RESERVOIR: a body of water stored for public use

ARE YOU A CITY MOUSE... OR A COUNTRY MOUSE?

Have you heard of these wonderful Wyoming town, city, or crossroad names? Perhaps you can start your own list!

MAJOR CITIES:

- Cheyenne
- Casper
- Laramie
- Rock Springs
- Green River
- Gillette

UNIQUE NAMES:

- Aladdin
- Bill
- Buffalo
- Cody
- Moose
- Muddy Gap
- Otto
- Rattlesnake Hills
- Smoot
- Story
- Wolf

Transportation

Major Interstate Highways

I-90

I-25

I-80

Railroads

Wyoming has 1,976 miles (3,180 kilometers) of railroad track.

Major Airports

Wyoming has 142 airports, many of them private airfields. The major cities are served by airports, although none of them are considered busy by national standards.

Timeline

1743 French Canadians François and Louis Joseph Vérendrye become the first known whites to enter present-day Wyoming

1803 Louisiana Purchase grants most of Wyoming to the U.S.

1834 William Sublette and Robert Campbell build Fort William (later renamed Fort Laramie)

1847 Brigham Young leads Mormon followers through Wyoming along the Mormon Trail to Utah

1866 Fort Phil Kearny and Fort Reno are established to protect travelers

1867 Union Pacific Railroad enters Wyoming; Cheyenne is founded

1868 Congress establishes Wyoming Territory

1872 Congress establishes Yellowstone National Park as the nation's first national park

1883 Buffalo Bill Cody begins his Wild West show

1887 Wyoming's capitol building is completed in Cheyenne

1890 Wyoming becomes the nation's 44th state

1906 Devils Tower becomes the first national monument

1924 Nellie Tayloe Ross is elected governor of Wyoming, becoming the nation's first woman governor

1960 F.E. Warren Air Force Base becomes the nation's first intercontinental ballistic missile base

1969 Wyoming's legislature passes a stiff severance tax on mineral extraction in the state

1988 Forest fires rage through Yellowstone National Park

1990 Centennial celebrations are held throughout the state

Here come the humans!

Thousands of years ago, ancient peoples inhabited Wyoming. They may have originally come across a frozen bridge of land between Asia and Alaska. If so, they slowly traveled east until some settled in what would one day become the state of Wyoming.

Throughout the state, scientists have found remains of ancient cultures. Arrowheads and spear points of the Early Hunters have been found, along with piles of mammoth bones. They are estimated to be more than 11,000 years old!

Native Americans Once Ruled!

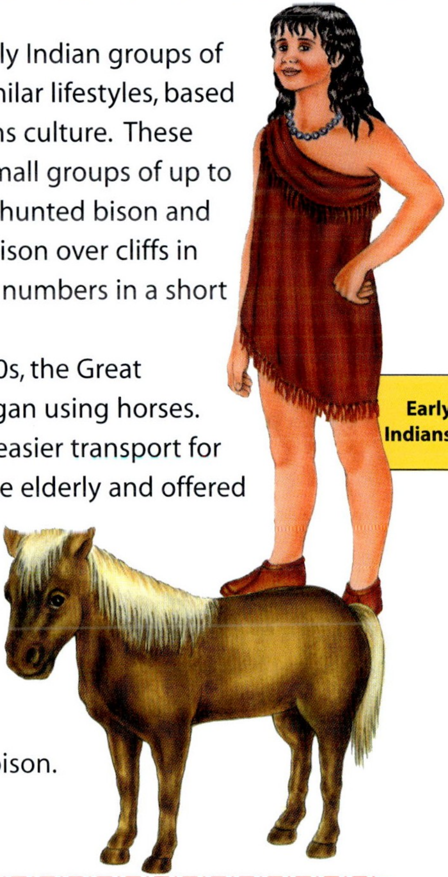

The various early Indian groups of Wyoming had similar lifestyles, based on the Great Plains culture. These Indians lived in small groups of up to 100 people. They hunted bison and often drove the bison over cliffs in order to kill large numbers in a short amount of time.

In the mid-1600s, the Great Plains Indians began using horses. Horses provided easier transport for the young and the elderly and offered greater mobility because they could carry more goods. Horses also enabled the Indians to more effectively hunt bison.

Word Definition

PISHKUN: high cliffs from which Indians would run groups of bison off of during a hunt

Land Ho!

Beaver lured the first white people to Wyoming in the mid-1700s. French, British, and American traders and trappers occupied Wyoming during this time. François and Louis Joseph de la Vérendrye were most likely the first white people to enter the state. They were in search of a trading route to the Pacific Ocean. Several other explorers, usually in search of abundant beavers, traveled through Wyoming.

After the Louisiana Purchase in 1803, President Thomas Jefferson sent Meriwether Lewis and William Clark to explore the little-known Rocky Mountain region. Although the two never entered Wyoming, their explorations paved the way for those to come.

Home, Sweet Home

Towns with permanent residents started popping up around Wyoming with the arrival of the railroad. Cheyenne and Laramie were two such towns. The first permanent white settlement in the state was Fort William (later renamed Fort Laramie).

Soon, railroads from both the east and west came. By 1869, the Union Pacific and Central Pacific railroads were connected and trains could run all the way from the Atlantic Ocean to the Pacific.

With their numbers growing, Wyomingites began to voice their desire to become an official U.S. territory. Their requests were honored on July 25, 1869. Cheyenne was declared the territorial capital and General John A. Campbell was appointed the territorial governor.

On December 10, 1869, the territorial legislature passed the nation's first act granting women the right to vote and hold public office.

Early Key Product

FURS

Early Key Product

Since beaver hats were all the rage in England, beaver furs brought in a high price in the mid-1700s. Trappers and traders were quick to reach Wyoming to be a part of the successful fur trade. Many businessmen organized fur companies and hired trappers and traders. The Rocky Mountain Fur Company, American Fur Company, and the North West Company were a few of these companies.

In 1825, the first fur trappers' rendezvous was held at Henrys Fork of the Green River. Rocky Mountain trappers from all over would assemble and swap tales and important information, as well as furs, knives, and guns.

The fur trade began to decline around 1840. Overtrapping had thinned out the beaver population, and beaver hats were going out of style.

Oregon Trail

Thomas J. Farnham was the first of many pioneers to head out across Wyoming for the fertile farmland of Oregon. He and his pack horses made the trip in 1839, followed by a group of about 30 people in 1841. Their wagon wheels made ruts in the land, thus providing a "trail" for others to follow. In the next few years, thousands of pioneers followed the Oregon Trail across Wyoming.

Mormon Trail

Members of the Church of Latter-day Saints, also known as Mormons, became the next wave of pioneers. Mormon leader Brigham Young led a train of followers in ox-drawn wagons across Wyoming and into Utah along what was called the Mormon Trail. The Mormons were fleeing religious persecution in the East. In the years to come, thousands of Mormons made the trip by foot, pulling handcarts. By 1869, around 85,000 Mormons had traveled the trail!

Freedom! Freedom!

While Wyoming was being explored and harvested for furs, settlers in the East were growing upset with their mother country, England. They felt that England ignored their ideas and concerns and taxed them too heavily.

Revolution

In 1775, the American colonies went to war with England. This war was called the American Revolution, or the Revolutionary War. On July 4, 1776, the Declaration of Independence was signed, cutting ties with England. In 1783, the war ended and the colonies became the United States of America.

Slaves and Slavery

Early in eastern U.S. history, Africans were brought to work on plantations. Thousands of slaves were made to work on these large farms, growing and harvesting crops. Over time, some states abolished slavery, while others (many southern states) became more dependent on slavery. The fighting between the abolitionists and the slaveowners continued to mount. At this time, Wyoming was not a state—it was a territory. Rather than ease the nation's problems regarding slavery, the Western Territories only increased the arguments. The Supreme Court's *Dred Scott* v. *Sanford* decision made slavery legal in all territories. This angered the abolitionists. These events and feelings eventually led to the Civil War.

In 1865, the 13th Amendment abolished slavery in the United States.

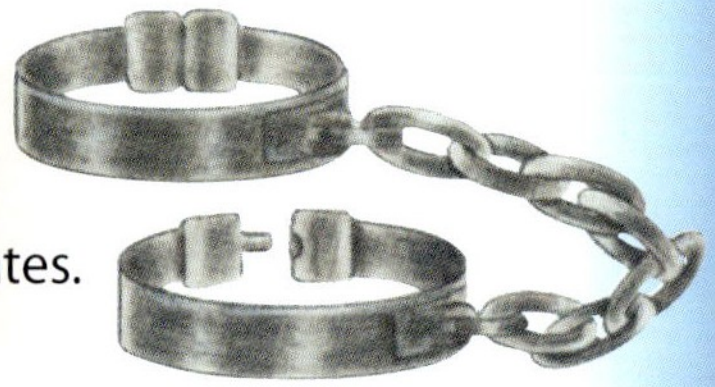

Word Definition

ABOLITIONIST: person who believed slavery was wrong and should be ended

The Civil War

Brother

The Civil War was fought between the American states. The argument was over states' rights to make their own decisions, including whether or not to own slaves. Some of the southern states began to secede (leave) the Union. They formed the Confederate States of America. At the time of the Civil War, Wyoming was not yet a state, it was a part of the Western Territories. Wyoming Territory was not established until 1868, three years after the end of the Civil War.

Word Definition

RECONSTRUCTION: the recovery and rebuilding period following the Civil War

vs. Brother

The Civil War was also called the War Between the States. Soldiers often found themselves fighting against former friends and neighbors, even brother against brother. Those who did survive often went home without an arm, leg, or both, since amputation was the "cure" for most battlefield wounds. More Americans were killed during the Civil War than during World Wars I and II together!

Army troops stationed in Wyoming were called to fight in the Civil War, and their absence caused Indian attacks to increase.

Get It In Writing!

1776
Declaration of Independence

1789
U.S. Constitution

1803
Louisiana Purchase gives most of Wyoming to the U.S.

1869
Woman Suffrage Bill

1890
State constitution ratified

WELCOME TO AMERICA!

People have come to Wyoming from other states and many other countries on almost every continent! As time goes by, Wyoming's population grows more diverse. This means that people of different races and from different cultures and ethnic backgrounds have moved to Wyoming.

In the past, many immigrants have come to Wyoming from Italy, Greece, Germany, China, Ireland, and Mexico. More recently, immigrants from Vietnam, Korea, and Japan have also settled in Wyoming. Only a certain number of immigrants are allowed to move to America each year. Many of these immigrants eventually become U.S. citizens.

1886-87

Severe winter kills many cattle

1926-30

Drought and Great Depression cause hardships throughout the state

Disasters & Catastrophes!

1979

Tornado kills one, injures 40; hits 500 homes in an 8-mile (13-kilometer) path across northern Cheyenne

1988

Fires rage through Yellowstone National Park

Giddy-Up!

The Pony Express of the Wild West got its start in St. Joseph, Missouri, on April 3, 1860. The boys of the Pony Express carried mail on horseback from St. Joseph to Sacramento, California, crossing through Wyoming. They would change horses every few miles so that they could cross the country in around 10 days!

Daring and highly skilled, the Pony Express riders braved all kinds of weather, difficult routes, hostile Indians, and vicious wolves to carry out their task. Famous Wyomingite "Buffalo Bill" Cody was one of these brave riders.

The Pony Express only lasted about a year and a half, then was put out of business with the creation of the transcontinental telegraph. It is remembered as one of the United States' great endeavors.

Wyoming Women

1869

Territorial legislature passes the nation's first woman suffrage bill

1870

Esther Hobart Morris is appointed justice of the peace in South Pass City, becoming the nation's first female judge; Eliza Swain becomes the first woman in the nation to cast a vote in a general election

1894

Estelle Reel is voted Wyoming's superintendent of education, becoming the first woman in the nation to hold a state elective office

1924

Nellie Tayloe Ross is elected governor of Wyoming, becoming the nation's first woman governor

Fight! Fight! Fight!

Wars that impacted Wyoming include:

- Revolutionary War
- War of 1812
- Indian War
- Mormon War
- Civil War
- World War I
- World War II
- Korean War
- Vietnam War
- Persian Gulf War

Magnificent Yellowstone

John Colter was the first white man to explore the Yellowstone and Grand Teton park regions. Colter spent the fall and winter of 1807–08 exploring the wonders of this area. Perhaps Colter realized what a magnificent treasure he had found in the amazing Rockies, the abundant wildlife, and the spectacular streams and canyons of Yellowstone.

Magnificent Yellowstone

In 1872, Yellowstone National Park became the country's first national park. It houses 10,000 thermal features such as hot, bubbling mineral pools, mudpots and mud volcanoes, and geysers. Geysers are streams of hot water that shoot into the sky. There are more geysers in Yellowstone than anywhere else in the world. The most famous geyser is Old Faithful.

The Yellowstone River's Upper and Lower falls cascade through the beautiful Grand Canyon of the Yellowstone. Several different places offer scenic views of the falls and the gray, pink, and purple canyon walls.

Indian Tribes

Cheyenne
Arapaho
Sioux
Blackfoot
Crow
Shoshone
Bannock

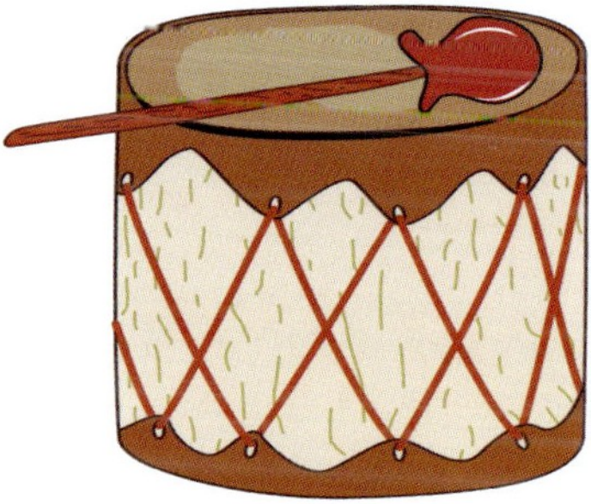

Other tribes who at one time hunted in Wyoming include the Ute, Flathead, Nez Percé, and the Kiowa.

Some Indian tribes began migrating west to the Great Plains as white settlers took their land. As the plains became more populated, rivalries grew intense among different Native American groups.

The Indians of Wyoming could not have known that the coming of the white man would mean an end to the way of life they had known for hundreds of years.

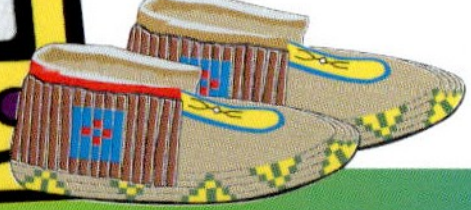

Here, There, Everywhere!

Jim Bridger—trapper, scout; explored Rocky Mountains

Benjamin Louis Eulalie de Bonneville—Army officer, explorer; explored Rocky Mountains, Green River area; found oil in Wind River Basin

John Colter—took part in Lewis and Clark expedition; first white person to travel through Yellowstone Park region

John Charles Frémont—soldier, explorer, politician

William Lewis Sublette—mountain man, trapper, explorer

David Jackson—explorer; Jackson Hole is named after him

Ferdinand Vandeveer Hayden—geologist; explored Rocky Mountains; urged that Yellowstone become a national park

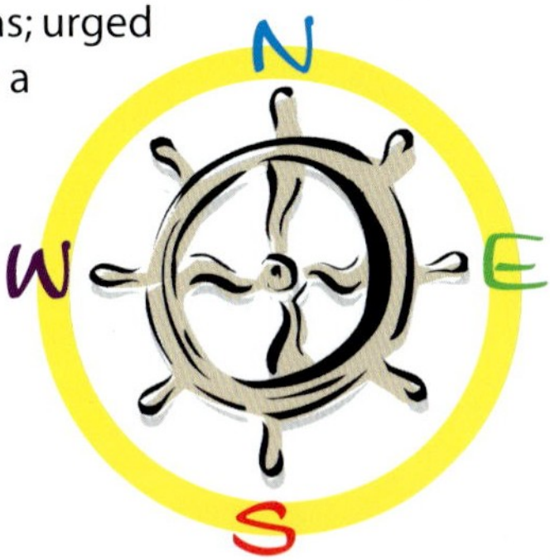

Founding Fathers

Joseph M. Carey—judge, politician; organized the Wyoming Development Company in 1885 to bring water to the Wheatland area; as a U.S. senator, introduced the Wyoming Statehood bill and wrote the 1894 Carey Act which enabled more homesteaders to settle in Wyoming

General John A. Campbell—territorial governor

Edgar Wilson Nye—served on territorial legislature; Laramie's postmaster and justice of the peace

Founding Mothers

"Grandma" Eliza Swain—first woman in American history to vote in a general election

Mary G. Bellamy—first female state legislator

Famous Native Americans

Sacajawea—Shoshone Indian woman who served as a guide for the Lewis and Clark expedition; later married a Comanche Indian in Oklahoma; returned to Wyoming to live with the Shoshone in the 1840s; said to be buried west of Fort Washakie

Washakie—Shoshone Indian leader; spent much of his life in Wyoming; fought for land and protection for his people and helped the Army in battles against the Sioux; signed the 1868 Treaty of Fort Bridger, allowing railroads to be built through Shoshone lands; buried on Wind River Indian Reservation with military honors, the first ever bestowed on an Indian chief

Red Cloud—Sioux chief; went on warpath against settlers for trespassing on Indian lands; led the Fetterman Massacre with Crazy Horse, killing 81 white men

Spotted Tail—Sioux chief; urged compromise to avoid violence with settlers; key player in his nephew Crazy Horse's surrender to the U.S.; shot by one of his own men for political reasons

Ghosts

DID SOMEONE SAY BOO!?

Hotel Haunt

A third-floor room is supposedly haunted at the Sheridan Inn in Sheridan. Cold spots have been felt and soft footsteps can be heard.

Monster in the Mist

Indians in the area of Lake de Smet believe an evil monster rises from a mist in the lake. This creature has been blamed for several drowning deaths.

White Devil

On the Rattlesnake Range in Casper there have been reports of a white stallion, called "White Devil," that tries to protect herds of wild mustangs by attacking and chasing off cowboys.

DO YOU BELIEVE IN GHOSTS?

Mountain Men

The "mountain man" is one of the most recognized figures in western history. Wyoming had its share of these daring men. They blazed trails, discovered mountain passes, mapped land and water routes, and learned about unfamiliar plants and animals.

Jim Bridger was considered one of the finest mountain men of the West. He built Fort Bridger in southwest Wyoming to serve as a supply post for travelers along westbound trails. He was often called the "Daniel Boone of the Rockies." After one long and winding trip through the wilderness, Bridger said, "I wasn't lost; I just didn't know where I was for a couple of weeks."

Jedediah Strong Smith was a fur trader. He discovered the South Pass through the Rocky Mountains, a gateway to the Far West.

Jim Beckwourth and **Edward Rose** were two black mountain men who were experts at trapping. They were well-known as excellent guides and scouts also.

Champion Rider

Wyoming has always been known for its cowboys and rodeos. One of their favorite hometown boys is Chris LeDoux. Beginning the rodeo at the young age of 14, LeDoux participated in (and won!) many national championship titles in bareback riding. In 1976, LeDoux won the title of World Champion Bareback Rider.

LeDoux is not only an excellent rider, he is also a talented songwriter and singer. In 1980, he left the rodeo to focus on his music career.

Champion Wrestler

Wyoming is known for cowboys and rodeos, but what about wrestlers? As the underdog at the 2000 Sydney Olympics, Rulon Gardner of Afton, Wyoming, competed against Alexander Karelin, the "Russian Bear," in Greco-Roman wrestling. Rulon defeated Karelin, who held the championship title for the past 13 years, to win the gold. Perhaps the title "Wyoming Bison" is fitting for the 286-pound (130-kilogram) Rulon!

Authors

- **June Etta Downey**—author and poet
- **Bill Nye**—journalist, humorist; collections of columns published in many books including *Bill Nye's History of the U.S.*
- **Maxwell Struthers Burt**—novelist; books include *In the High Hills, Diary of a Dude Wrangler,* and *Powder River*
- **Peggy Simpson Curry**—novelist; books include *Fire in the Water, Red Wind of Wyoming, So Far from Spring,* and *The Oil Patch*
- **Taft Alfred Larson**—educator, historian, professor, author; authority on Wyoming history; author of four books on Wyoming history

- **Caroline Lockhart**—journalist, novelist; seven famous novels are all based on Cody characters
- **Ted Olson**—poet; began his writing career as a journalist in Laramie

- **Owen Wister**—novelist; experiences in Wyoming provided much of the material for his novel *The Virginian;* other works include *Red Men and White* and *The Pentecost of Calamity*

Artists

Jackson Pollock—abstract impressionist painter

Harry Andrew Jackson—sculptor; his many one-person shows have included an exhibit at the Smithsonian Institution; many works are permanent collections in museums across the U.S.; commissioned to make the bronze Sacajawea monument at the Plains Indian Museum

Thomas Moran—English-born artist; traveled with surveying party in the 1870s, making sketches of scenery, which he later developed into paintings; Mount Moran, in the Teton range, is named for him

Robert Isaiah Russin—sculptor; professor of art at the University of Wyoming; his sculpture *The Family* stands on the University of Wyoming campus

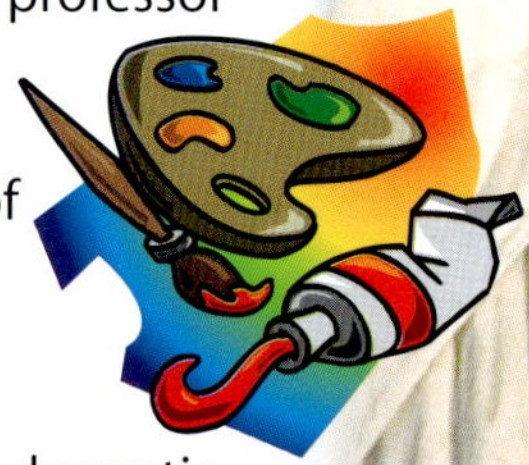

Ansel Adams—photographer; captured Wyoming's grandeur in dramatic black-and-white photographs

Entertainers

Harrison Ford—actor; first famous for roles in *Star Wars* and *Raiders of the Lost Ark;* moved to Wyoming in the 1980s to escape the hustle and bustle of Hollywood

Isabel Jewell—movie star; starred in *Mad Love* and *Go West Young Man*

Chris LeDoux—rodeo champion; country music star

Curt Gowdy—sportscaster; covered Boston Red Sox games, National Football League games, Super Bowls, and World Series; hosted ABC's *Wide World of Sports* and *American Sportsman*

Devils Tower is well known to those who have seen the movie *Close Encounters of the Third Kind.* It is the spot where an alien spaceship lands.

Very Important People

James Cash Penney—founder of the J.C. Penney stores

June Etta Downey—psychologist, author; pioneer in the study of personality; researched imagination and creativity, color blindness, and handwriting

William "Buffalo Bill" Cody—frontiersman, scout, Indian fighter, showman; rode for Pony Express; earned the nickname "Buffalo Bill" while hunting bison to feed railroad crews; organized a traveling show called Buffalo Bill's Wild West Show, which gained international fame; founded the town of Cody

Grace Raymond Hebard—historian, librarian, educator; became a professor at University of Wyoming; conducted research and wrote numerous books on Wyoming and Western history; campaigned for woman suffrage

Gerald Spence—lawyer, writer; one of the nation's top trial lawyers; won some of the biggest court judgments in history

Political Leaders

Dick Cheney—U.S. representative from Wyoming; chief of staff to President Gerald Ford; U.S. secretary of defense under President George Bush; vice president under President George W. Bush

Nellie Tayloe Ross—nation's first woman governor (1924); finished her deceased husband's term as governor; first female director of the U.S. Mint

Alan Simpson—state legislator; U.S. senator; as senator, led immigration reform

Francis Emroy Warren—Civil War veteran; governor of Wyoming; U.S. senator for 37 years

Esther Morris—mother of women's suffrage in Wyoming; active in winning the right to vote for women in Wyoming; first female justice of the peace in the U.S.

Harriet Elizabeth Byrd—Wyoming state representative and state senator; worked to establish Martin Luther King, Jr. Day as a state holiday

Edward Herschler—lawyer; served three terms as governor of Wyoming

Willis Van Devanter—lawyer; judge; chief justice of Wyoming Territory; U.S. circuit judge; U.S. Supreme Court justice

Bandits & Outlaws

Trains and stagecoaches were easy prey for outlaws. They knew there were never enough soldiers and lawmen to cover all of the trails and tracks the stagecoaches and trains traveled. Wyoming had its fair share of train and stagecoach robberies by notorious bandits and outlaws.

"Big Nose" George Parrott would hide out near Sheridan when he robbed the Deadwood Stage. The infamous outlaw brothers, **Frank and Jesse James**, would also hide out there.

One of the most notorious gangs was the "Wild Bunch," led by **Butch Cassidy** and Harry Longbaugh, better known as the **Sundance Kid**. The gang's favorite hideout was southwest of Kaycee, a place called Red Canyon, or Hole-in-the-Wall. Gang members would leave messages for each other on the canyon walls.

Keeping the Faith

First Methodist Church, Cheyenne—second home of this congregation; first home was the famous site of the 1876 wedding of Wild Bill Hickok and a lady circus rider

Saint Matthew's Episcopal Cathedral, Laramie

Chapel of Transfiguration, Moose—one-room log chapel, well known for its view of the Tetons seen through the window behind the altar

Saint Michael's Mission, Ethete—established by the Episcopal missionary church and the Arapaho

SCHOOLS

University of Wyoming, Laramie—only 4-year institution of higher learning in the state

Casper College

Eastern Wyoming College, Torrington

Sheridan College

Northwest College, Powell

Central Wyoming College, Riverton

Western Wyoming College, Rock Springs

Laramie County Community College, Cheyenne

HISTORIC SITES

Independence Rock State Historic Landmark, near Casper—huge granite boulder where more than 5,000 emigrants along the Oregon Trail carved their names

Oregon Trail Ruts National Historic Landmark, near Guernsey

South Pass City State Historic Site—site of a gold-mining boomtown that sprang up in 1867

Medicine Wheel, near Lovell—circle of white, flat stones that may have been used as a calendar by prehistoric Indians

Father De Smet Prairie Mass Site, Daniel—marks where the Belgian priest celebrated Wyoming's first Catholic mass

PARKS

Yellowstone National Park, Wyoming's northwestern corner

Grand Teton National Park, south of Yellowstone National Park

Home, Sweet Home!

Historic Governor's Mansion, Cheyenne—home of Wyoming's governors from 1904 to 1976

Jim Baker Cabin, Savery—built in 1873 by the well-known trapper and scout

Pahaska Tepee, east of Yellowstone—log cabin of William "Buffalo Bill" Cody; served as a hunting lodge

Miller Cabin, Jackson—two cabins; homestead of Robert Miller, who laid out the town of Jackson

Bath Home, Laramie—built in 1875 by Henry Bath, a German immigrant and early cattle rancher

Ferris Mansion, Rawlins—built in 1903 for George Ferris, an early mining figure

J.C. Penney's Home, Kemmerer—clapboard house where J.C. Penney moved his family after living in his store building

A few of Wyoming's famous Battles

- **Mormon War,** Green River Valley—conflict between U.S. troops and Mormons
- **Battle of Tongue River,** near Montana border—General Patrick Connor charged Cheyenne and Arapaho villages
- **Wagon Box Fight of 1867,** near Fort Phil Kearny—timber-cutting crew fended off Sioux and Cheyenne warriors from behind their overturned wagons

A few of Wyoming's famous Forts

- **Fort Fred Steele,** Medicine Bow—designed to protect railroad work crews and settlers; also was a supply depot for troops fighting the Plains Indians
- **Fort Bridger**—trading post built in 1842 by Jim Bridger; served as an important stopover for westward-bound emigrants
- **Fort Laramie,** northwest of Torrington—site of Wyoming's first military post, established to protect travelers along Oregon Trail
- **Fort Phil Kearny,** north of Buffalo—site of the 1866 fort that protected the Bozeman Trail
- **Fort Yellowstone**—established to enforce rules of the national park, including catching poachers and fighting forest fires
- **Fort Washakie**—built at the request of Shoshone chief Washakie when he agreed to move his people onto the Wind River Reservation

Libraries

Check out the following special Wyoming libraries! (Do you have a library card? Have you worn it out yet?!)

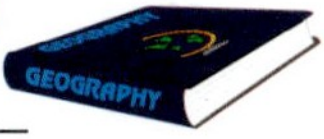

William Robertson Coe Library, Laramie—part of the University of Wyoming

Wyoming State Library, Cheyenne—houses a fine collection of law books

McCracken Research Library, Cody—part of the Buffalo Bill Historical Center

Jackson Research Library—jointly operated by the University of Wyoming and the National Park Service

Albany County Library, Laramie

Attractions

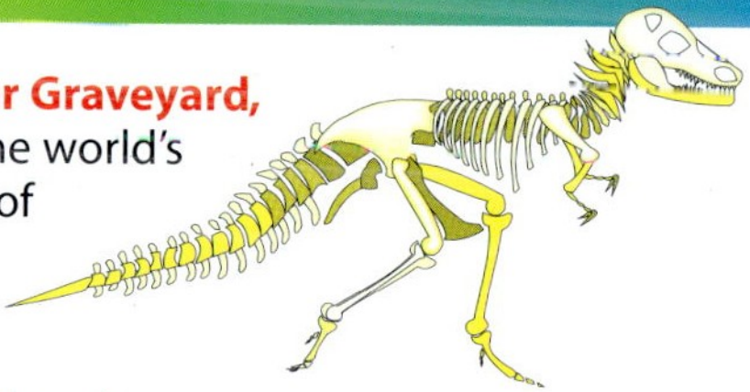

Como Bluff Dinosaur Graveyard, Rock River—site of the world's first major discovery of dinosaur remains, unearthed in 1877

Bighorn Canyon National Recreation Area, northern Wyoming—scenic area of colorful, fossil-filled cliffs

Flaming Gorge National Recreation Area, south of Green River—201,000-acre (81,343-hectare) scenic wilderness, including rock formations, canyons, and deserts

Wind River Canyon, between Shoshone and Thermopolis—layered cliffs show successive eras in Wyoming's geological history

Castle Garden Petroglyphs, Riverton—prehistoric drawings on sandstone cliffs; their meaning remains a mystery

Buffalo Bill Historical Center, Cody—contains the boyhood home, statue, and museum of the famous Buffalo Bill Cody

First J.C. Penney Store, Kemmerer—first called the Golden Rule Store; opened in 1902

Museums

Cheyenne Frontier Days Old West Museum

F.E. Warren Military Museum, Cheyenne

Wyoming State Museum, Cheyenne

Grand Encampment Museum, Encampment—preserves a number of buildings from the 1890s copper-mining town

Museum of the Mountain Men, Pinedale

Wyoming Pioneer Memorial Museum, Douglas

Homesteaders Museum, Torrington

Stagecoach Museum, Lusk

Explorer's Museum, Yellowstone National Park at Madison's Junction

Colter Bay Indian Arts Museum, Moose

Jackson Hole Museum, Jackson

Winchester Arms Museum, Cody

Lest We Forget

Fort Sanders Monument, Laramie—stone memorial marking the site of the fort

Rock Springs Stage Station Monument

Devils Tower National Monument, near Sundance—tower of volcanic rock; first national monument

Fossil Butte National Monument, near Kemmerer—contains the world's largest and most diverse deposits of fossilized fish

Washakie's Grave, Fort Washakie—final resting place of Shoshone Indian chief who worked for peace with the settlers; only Indian chief known to have received full military burial rites

Grave of Sacajawea, Fort Washakie—historians dispute this location as the grave site of the Shoshone Indian guide of the Lewis and Clark expedition

The Arts

Whitney Gallery of Western Art, Cody

Nicolaysen Art Museum, Casper—highlights both regional and national contemporary artists

Wildlife of the American West Art Gallery, Jackson—houses the finest collection of wildlife art in the world

Cheyenne Symphony Orchestra

Casper Civic Symphony Orchestra

Wyoming's Western Arts Trio—performs in Laramie, Cheyenne, and Saratoga

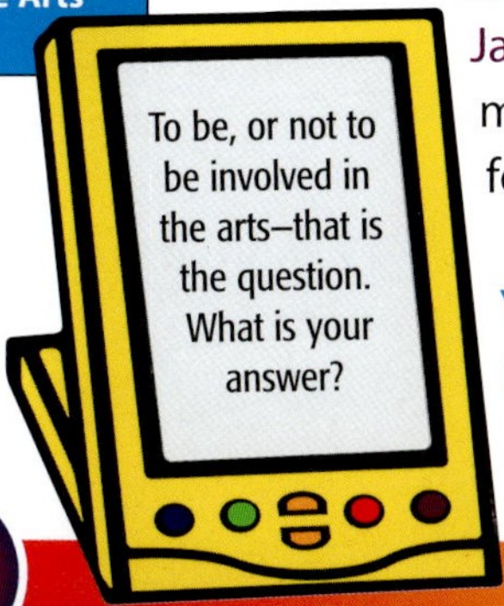

Grand Teton Music Festival, Jackson Hole—Wyoming's most extravagant music festival

Yellowstone Jazz Festival, Cody

Devils Tower

Rising up out of the flat land around it, Devils Tower is an awesome sight to behold. This ancient volcano thrusts up 1,267 feet (386 meters) above the Belle Fourche River. Some Indian tribes called it "Bad God's Tower." Colonel Richard Dodge adapted that name and called it "Devils Tower."

One Indian legend says the formation was created when seven maidens were playing nearby and woke a slumbering bear. Trying to flee the bear, the maidens were rescued when a rock they climbed upon rose higher and higher, out of the bear's reach. The bear attempted to reach the maidens by clawing at the rock tower, which is why there are fluted marks on the side of Devils Tower!

Devils Tower

On July 4, 1893, two local men were the first to climb to the top. Today, over 1,000 climbers reach the summit each year. In 1906, President Teddy Roosevelt declared Devils Tower the nation's first national monument.

Roads

John D. Rockefeller, Jr. Memorial Parkway, south from Yellowstone into Grand Tetons—scenery is breathtaking

North Fork of the Shoshone, east entrance of Yellowstone to Cody—includes Chimney Rock, Shoshone National Forest, and the Buffalo Bill Historical Center

Big Horn Mountains Scenic Byway, Dayton to Shell—travels through river valleys, across rolling meadows, and dives into dazzling gorges

Snowy Range Road, Laramie to Saratoga—one of the most spectacular drives in the state

Centennial Scenic Byway, Dubois to Pinedale—passes nearly every major sight in the region—the Snake River, Grand Tetons, Wind River Range, and the Green River Valley

and More!

Bozeman Trail—built by John Bozeman for westward travelers; running from Colorado to Montana, it crossed through Wyoming's Powder River Basin; known as the "Bloody Bozeman" because of the dozens of battles with Indians that occurred along the trail

Hot Springs!

Thermopolis is home to the largest hot springs in the world! These hot springs gush 18,600,000 gallons (70,408,000 liters) of water a day. The water of Big Horn Spring is hot—128°F (53°C)! Its overspill has created terraces brightly colored with algae in various shades of yellow, red, and orange. The steaming mineral waters are channeled to both public and private swimming pools and bathhouses. Even in the frigid cold of winter, these swimming pools are open to bathers. Imagine the sight—falling snowflakes, clouds of steam, bathing suits, and cowboy hats!

Hot Springs State Park near Thermopolis became Wyoming's first state park.

SOME OF WYOMING'S ANIMALS INCLUDE:

Pronghorn Antelope
White-tailed Deer
Mule Deer
Badgers
Moose
Lynxes
Black Bear
Grizzly Bear

Beavers
Bison
Coyotes
Rabbits
Elk
Ferrets
Foxes

Rocky Mountain Goats
Bobcats
Chipmunks

Otters
Raccoons
Mountain Lions
Prairie Dogs

The largest herd of pronghorn antelope in the world live in Wyoming.

Take a Walk on the Wild Side!

Wyoming is home to more than 600 species of animals. However abundant in number of species, they still have a few animals that are considered endangered or threatened in the state.

Some endangered Wyoming animals are:

Whooping Crane
Peregrine Falcon
Blackfooted Ferret
Wyoming Toad
Gray Wolf
Grizzly Bear

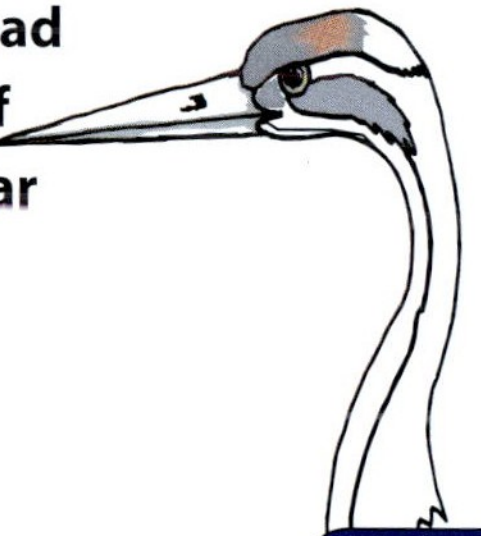

The National Elk Refuge in Jackson Hole is the winter home of thousands of elk.

Birds

You may spy these birds in Wyoming:

Chickadees
Grouse
Cranes
Partridges
Doves
Ducks
Bald Eagles
Golden Eagles
Prairie Falcons
Geese
Hawks
Ospreys
Warblers
Mockingbirds
Orioles
Owls
Sparrows
Brown Thrashers
Wild Turkeys
Woodpeckers

The trumpeter swan, once nearly extinct, can be found in Yellowstone and Grand Teton National Parks.

Don't let these Wyoming bugs bug you!

Mayfly
Cricket
Water Bug
Spittlebug
Whirligig Beetle
Weevil
Moth

Bumblebee

Ants

Monarch Butterfly

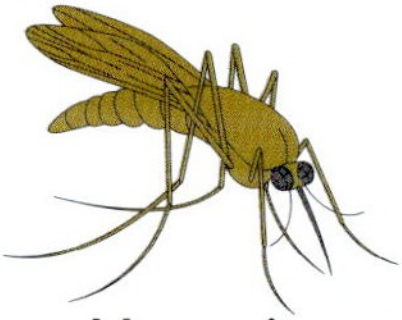

Mosquito

Honeybee

Dragonfly

Ladybug

Grasshopper

Whirligig beetles have two pairs of eyes—one pair looks above the water, the other under it!

Fish

Swimming in Wyoming's waters:

- Brook Trout
- Cutthroat Trout
- Rainbow Trout
- Brown Trout
- Bass
- Walleye
- Crappie
- Perch
- Channel Catfish

Pond Critters

In Wyoming's ponds, you may find:

Hydra
Leech
Freshwater Mussel
Freshwater Crayfish
Fishing Spider
Dragonfly
Diving Beetle
Muskrat

Rocks and Minerals

Minerals are the building blocks of all rocks. Most minerals are tiny and you need a magnifying glass to see them clearly. Some minerals you may find in Wyoming include:

Iron Pyrite
Quartz
Calcite
Feldspar
Kaolinite
Mica
Hornblende

Rocks are solid masses of minerals or rock fragments that occur in nature. Some rocks you may find in Wyoming include:

Tuff
Sandstone
Shale
Gneiss
Coal
Slate

TREEMENDOUS!

THESE TREES TOWER OVER WYOMING:

ALDER
ASH
LIMBER PINE
PONDEROSA PINE
YELLOW PINE
WHITE PINE
ALPINE FIR
DOUGLAS FIR
ASPEN
BIRCH
MOUNTAIN MAHOGANY
COTTONWOOD
HAWTHORN
POPLAR
WHITEBARK
WILLOW

Wildflowers

Are you crazy about these Wyoming wildflowers?

- Violet
- Trillium
- Wild Geranium
- Columbine
- Lady's Slipper
- Jacob's Ladder
- Spring Beauty
- Black-eyed Susan
- Indian Paintbrush
- Buttercup
- Butter-and-Eggs

Cream of the Crops

Agricultural products from Wyoming:

First/Big/Small/Etc.

The **federal government** owns one-half of the land in Wyoming.

The horse on the Wyoming license plate has a name, **"Old Steamboat,"** after a bucking bronco that was almost impossible to ride.

The **largest coal mine** in the U.S. is the Black Thunder mine in Wyoming.

The **first dude ranch** in Wyoming was the Eaton Ranch, near Dayton. The Eatons also came up with the term "dude."

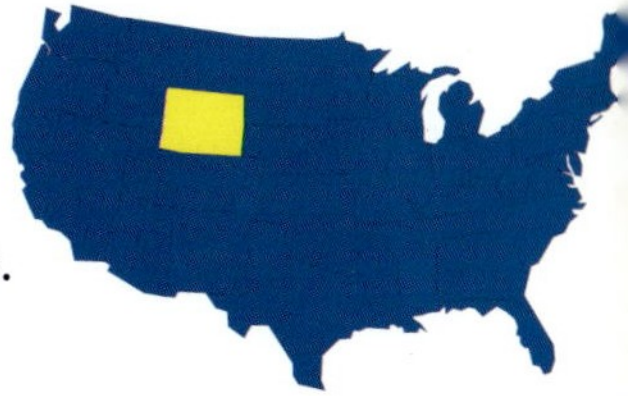

Wyoming has the **lowest population** of all 50 states.

The Indian name for Bull Lake was "the lake that roars." The **strange sound** comes from the wind blowing over the ice that forms on the lake during winter.

Festivals

Celebrate!!!

Wyoming's biggest celebration is Frontier Days, often called the "Daddy of 'Em All"! Thousands of people attend this celebration in Cheyenne the last full week of July. They enjoy pancake breakfasts and chili feasts, as well as carnival rides and air shows. The nearby Indian village run by the Shoshone tribe puts on displays of traditional Native American dancing and storytelling. However, the highpoint of Frontier Days is the rodeo, the oldest in the United States! Rodeo contests include bronco and steer riding, roping calves and steers, and barrel racing. Both men and women compete in the rodeo.

Other Wyoming festivals:

Jackalope Day Celebration, Douglas

Wyoming State Fair, Douglas

Medicine Bow Days

Green River Rendezvous, Pinedale

Holidays

Calendar

Groundhog Day, *February 2*	Presidents' Day, *3rd Monday in February*	St. Patrick's Day, *March 17*
Memorial Day, *last Monday in May*	Independence Day, *July 4*	Labor Day, *1st Monday in September*
Columbus Day *2nd Monday in October*	Veterans Day, *November 11*	Thanksgiving, *4th Thursday in November*

Wyoming celebrates its admission to the U.S. on July 10.

Christmas, Chanukah, Kwanzaa, Vietnamese Tet, and Chinese New Year are all special celebrations in Wyoming.

WYOMING IS FAMOUS FOR . . .

THE FOLLOWING FOODS!

- Buttermilk Pie
- Barbecued Beef
- Elk Steak
- Cowboy Biscuits and Ice Cream
- Bison Burger
- Grilled Trout
- Broiled Walleye
- Chuckwagon Beans
- Home Fries
- Venison

Business & Trade

Wyoming Works!

Wyoming's manufacturing activities center around its minerals. Various manufacturing plants process coal, petroleum, iron ore, copper, and aluminum. Chemical plants manufacture fertilizers and other farm chemicals.

Factories in Wyoming produce a variety of nonelectrical machinery such as farm equipment, construction and oilfield equipment, and aeronautics equipment.

Food-processing plants across the state produce meat products, flour, beet sugar, cheese, and cattle feed.

Wyoming's third-largest industry is tourism. About 7 million people visit Wyoming every year! Tourism provides many jobs, but only seasonally.

Wyoming Books & Websites

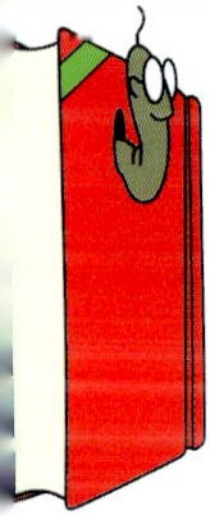

My First Book About Wyoming by Carole Marsh
America the Beautiful: Wyoming by Ann Heinrichs
Celebrate the States: Wyoming by Guy Baldwin
Let's Discover the States: Wyoming by the Aylesworths
The Wyoming Experience Series by Carole Marsh

Wyoming Glossary

Glossary Words

bandit: a robber; member of a gang of outlaws

bison: a large plains mammal; also known as buffalo

equality: balanced laws in terms of the rights of men and women

expedition: journey made for a specific purpose, as exploration

mammoth: large, prehistoric elephant; covered in hair and having large tusks

pioneer: a person who is among those who first enter or settle a region, opening it for more people to settle in

pishkun: high cliff

rendezvous: a meeting at a certain time and place

territory: a region of the U.S. not admitted as a state, but having its own legislature and an appointed governor

Wyoming Spelling Bee

Here are some special Wyoming-related words to learn! To take the Spelling Bee, have someone call out the words and you spell them aloud or write them on a piece of paper.

SPELLING WORDS

Arapaho	petroglyph
bison	rendezvous
Cheyenne	reservation
equality	rodeo
explorer	Sacajawea
frontier	Shoshone
homesteader	Sioux
Laramie	traveler
lizard	triceratops
massacre	Washakie

ABOUT THE AUTHOR...

CAROLE MARSH has been writing about Wyoming for more than 20 years. She is the author of the popular *Wyoming State Stuff Series* for young readers and creator along with her son, Michael Marsh, of *Wyoming Facts and Factivities,* a CD-ROM widely used in Wyoming schools. The author of more than 100 Wyoming books and other supplementary educational materials on the state, Marsh is currently working on a new collection of Wyoming materials for young people. Marsh correlates her Wyoming materials to the Wyoming learning standards. Many of her books and other materials have been inspired by or requested by Wyoming teachers and librarians.

EDITORIAL ASSISTANT:

Jill Sanders

GRAPHIC DESIGNER:

Lisa Stanley